The **FIXER'S** Guide to...
AXLES

Written by **JOHN WOOD**

Designed by **AMY LI**

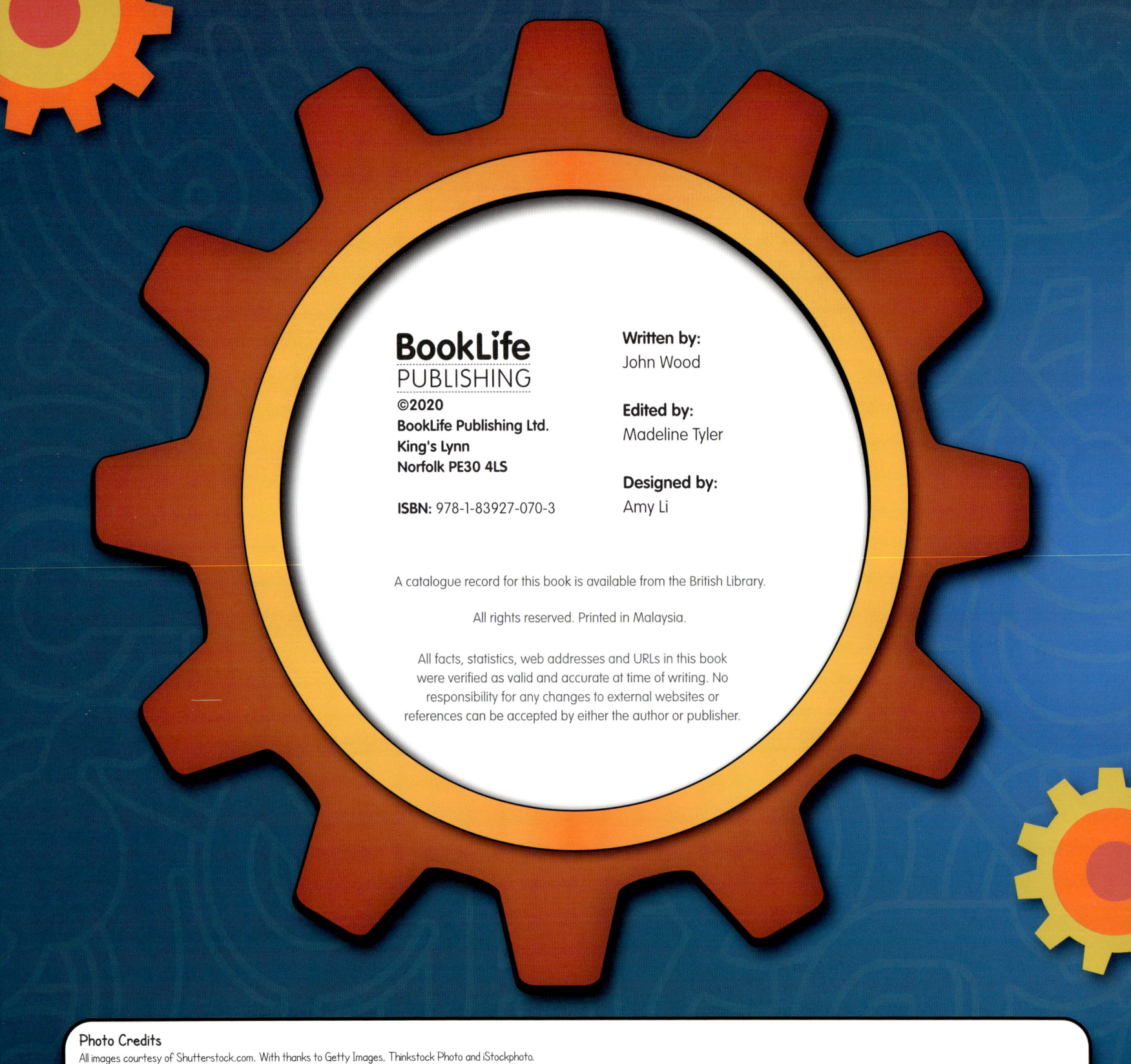

BookLife PUBLISHING

©2020
BookLife Publishing Ltd.
King's Lynn
Norfolk PE30 4LS

ISBN: 978-1-83927-070-3

Written by:
John Wood

Edited by:
Madeline Tyler

Designed by:
Amy Li

A catalogue record for this book is available from the British Library.

All rights reserved. Printed in Malaysia.

All facts, statistics, web addresses and URLs in this book were verified as valid and accurate at time of writing. No responsibility for any changes to external websites or references can be accepted by either the author or publisher.

Photo Credits

All images courtesy of Shutterstock.com. With thanks to Getty Images, Thinkstock Photo and iStockphoto.

Recurring images (cover and internals) — Guliveris (background pattern), Agor2012, robuart (cogs), Steve Paint (arrows), cover — Andrew Rybalko, aliaksei kruhlenia, Iconic Bestiary. 1 — Andrew Rybalko. 4–5 — Andrew Rybalko, Dmitry_Tsvetkov, Iconic Bestiary, mutsuMaks, Royalty-free stock vector, Andrii Bezvershenko. 6–7 — Stephen Gibson, Iconic Bestiary, Bilanol. 8–9 — Naypong Studio, Shamaan, Sviatlana Yankouskaya, rattanakk, Stockr, Svetlana Orusova, Zaitsava Olga. 10–11 — wavebreakmedia, VadimZosimov , Stock_VectorSale. 12–13 — Studio_G, Irina Danyliuk. 14–15 — Agor2012, Craig Russell, zhao jiankang. 16–17 — Agor2012, nuttanicha sadsanasuphin, gielmichal. 18–19 — HardtIllustrations, grmarc, NotionPic, Usagi-P, Royalty-free stock vector, Dmitry_Tsvetkov, Andrew Rybalko. 20–21 — HardtIllustrations, grmarc. 22–23 — NotionPic, grmarc, Usagi-P, Eva Speshneva.

CONTENTS

PAGE 4	Meet the Fixer
PAGE 6	Axles
PAGE 10	Parts of an Axle
PAGE 12	How an Axle Works
PAGE 14	Gears
PAGE 16	Big Gear, Little Gear
PAGE 18	Let's Build a Spinning Toy
PAGE 24	Glossary and Index

Words that look like this can be found in the glossary on page 24.

MEET THE FIXER

Oh no! Sorry about this mess — the Fixer can be a bit clumsy sometimes. Say sorry, Fixer.

Pfflbjullphtt.

Believe it or not, the Fixer is the smartest being in the universe when it comes to machines.

A machine is an object that makes a job easier to do. The Fixer wants to teach you about one of the simplest types of machine: an axle.

A watch is a machine. Even a pizza cutter is a simple machine.

AXLES

An axle is a thin, stiff rod that goes through the middle of a bigger, circular object called a wheel. The axle lets the wheel spin around.

Any wheel on a vehicle, such as a car or bike, has an axle.

Axle

Some axles are fixed to the wheels – when they turn, the wheel spins. Other axles stay still while the wheel spins around them.

Axles are everywhere. Here are a few examples.

In a wind turbine, the blades are the wheel, and the axle is in the middle.

Windmill

Wheelchair

A well has an axle. When it turns, it raises and lowers the bucket.

Thpluplelelepfl!

You're right, Fixer. There are some surprising axles on this page.

The handle of a tap is a wheel, and it is fixed to an axle. Turning the axle lets water flow out.

In a screwdriver, the handle is the wheel and the metal part is the axle.

There is an axle in the middle of some rolling pins.

PARTS OF AN AXLE

In a wheel and axle machine, there needs to be something to make it move. This might be a person, such as when someone pedals a bike. It could also be an <u>electric motor</u>.

In many vehicles, axles are turned by engines.

Axles also have bearings. Bearings are parts that go between the axle and wheel. They are used to take away <u>friction</u>, and they help the wheel or axle spin smoothly.

Many bearings are made up of small metal balls. These are called ball bearings.

Ball bearings

HOW AN AXLE WORKS

When a small, fixed axle is turned, it can turn a much bigger wheel. Axles let us spin wheels faster and easier.

Axles and wheels can spin either clockwise or anticlockwise.

Clockwise

Anticlockwise

Axles let us build machines that work harder, with wheels and gears that go faster. Wait, what are gears, Fixer?

BLEUBLUFFLE!

The Fixer says he is going to explain what gears are on the next page.

GEARS

A gear is a wheel which has teeth around the outside edge. The teeth help gears to fit together. When a gear turns around an axle, it also turns other gears that are connected to it.

Machines, such as clocks, can be made up of lots of gears.

A gear will always spin in the opposite direction of the gear turning it. This means that if the first gear is spinning clockwise, the second gear will spin anticlockwise.

Gears aren't always facing the same way. Gears can fit together in all sorts of ways.

BIG GEAR, LITTLE GEAR

When gears of different sizes are put together, they can change the speed and power of machines.

Turning a big gear once will make small gears turn lots of times. This will turn the axle more which gives you more speed.

Turning a little gear will make the big gear turn more slowly. However, this uses less force, so it is easier to turn.

Bicycles use different gears to help you pedal. It's easier to pedal in low gears because you're turning a small gear. Less force is needed to spin the wheels, but you will be slower.

Different sizes of gears on a bicycle

It's harder to pedal in high gears because you're turning a big gear. More force is needed, but you can be speedy.

LET'S BUILD A SPINNING TOY

It is time to build! We will be using axles to make a toy. It will have a part that spins when you turn the axle.

Pffflewueughh.

You will need to get an adult to help you when using the scissors and the glue.

YOU WILL NEED:

- Glue
- 2 bottlecaps
- 3 long, thin sticks of wood
- Scissors
- Colouring pens/pencils
- A straw
- A small cardboard box which is shorter and thinner than the sticks of wood
- A few small pieces of cardboard

Axle

STEP 1

Cut the front off your cardboard box.

STEP 2

Poke a hole in the top of your box and stick the straw through. Trim the straw and glue it in place.

STEP 3

Put a stick through the straw and glue a bottlecap to the end inside the box. Hold it in place while it dries.

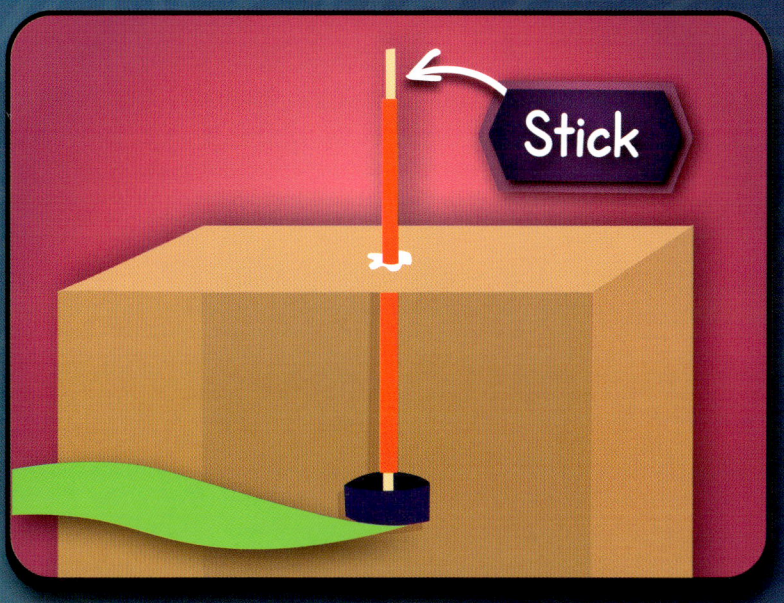

STEP 4

Using scissors, poke a hole through the other bottlecap.

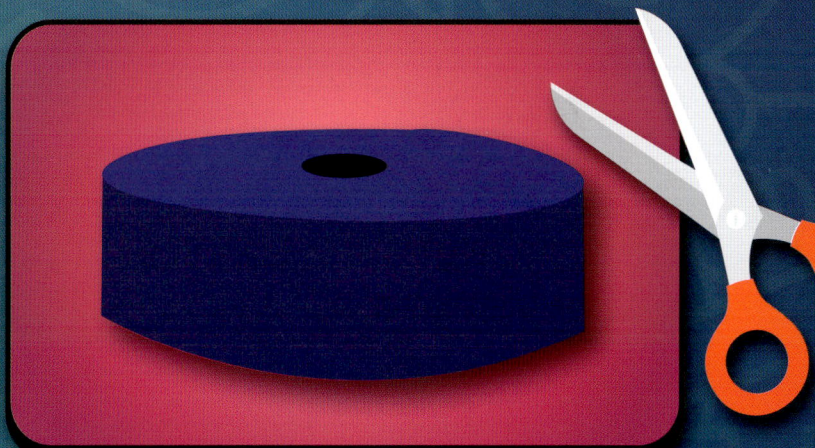

STEP 5

Push a stick through one side of the cardboard box, then through the bottlecap, then through the other side of the box. Keep the stick level, like in the picture.

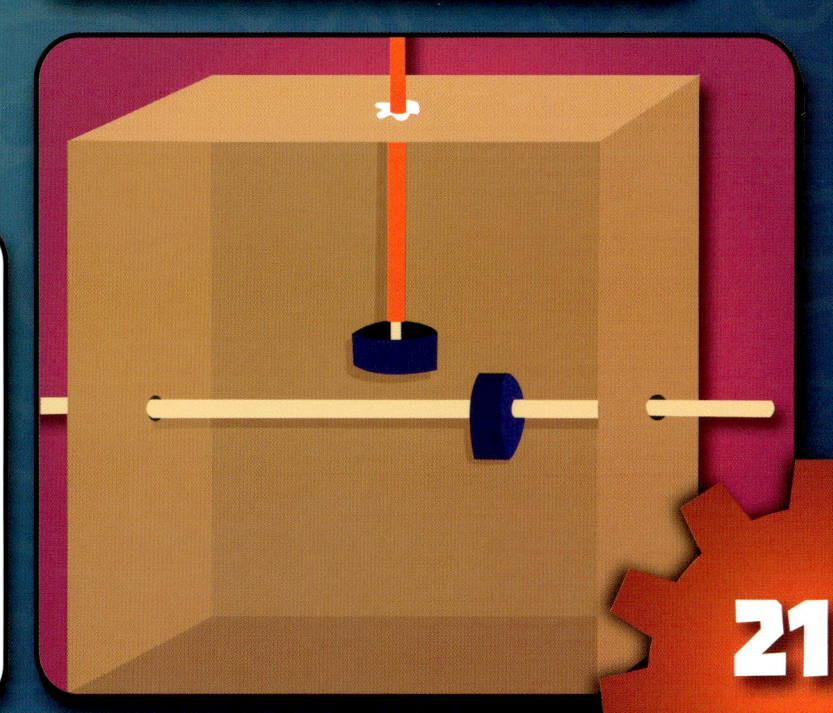

STEP 6

Slide the bottlecap along the stick until it is in the middle, and then glue it in place.

STEP 7

Make a handle for one end. First, glue a very small stick along one side of a square of cardboard. Glue the opposite side of the square to the end of the sideways stick.

STEP 8

Use your coloured pencils and other pieces of cardboard to create a character to spin around. It can be whatever you want!

STEP 9

Glue your character to the stick coming out of the top. Line the bottlecaps up like in the picture. Now turn the handle and watch your character spin.

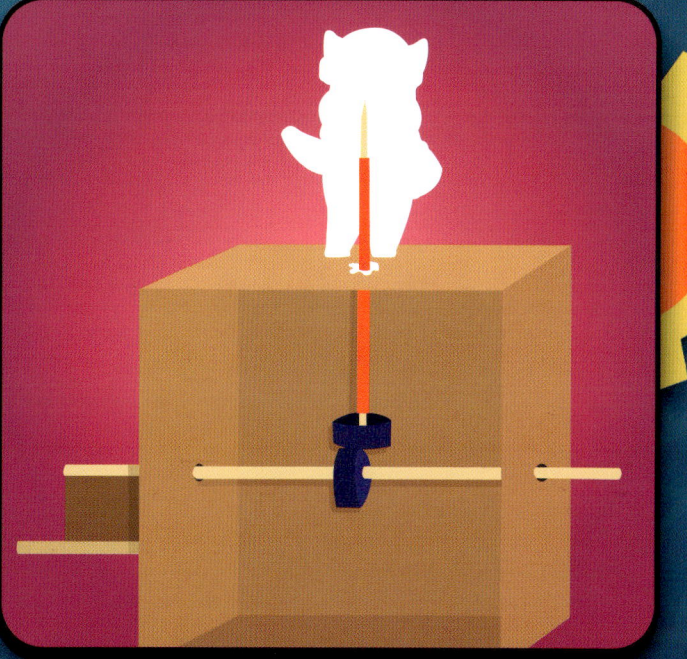

GLOSSARY

electric motor	machines that move things using electricity
force	a push or pull on an object
friction	a force that slows things down and creates heat when two things rub together
power	the ability something has to get things done
speed	how fast something goes
universe	the space that everything exists in, including planets, galaxies and stars
vehicle	a machine that has an engine and is used to carry people or things

INDEX

bearings 11
bikes 6, 10, 17
cars 6
electricity 10
friction 11
gears 13–17
machines 4–5, 10, 13–14, 16
pedalling 10, 17
speed 12–13, 16–17
spinning 6–7, 11–12, 15, 17–18, 23
wheels 6–14, 17